what is beautiful

honest poems for mothers
of small children

Sarah Dunning Park

PEACE HILL PRESS

The clothespin photo on the cover and title page was taken by
Jordi Payà Canals, an architect and photographer in Barcelona, used
via a Creative Commons Attribution-ShareAlike 2.0 Generic License
(CC BY-SA 2.0; http://creativecommons.org/licenses/by-sa/2.0/).
The original can be found at http://flickr.com/photos/arg0s/6864029455.
Contact Peace Hill Press for free access to the modified version used in this book.

The poems in this collection are set in Adobe Garamond Pro, a typeface
designed by Robert Slimbach, based on the work of the 16th century French
type designer Claude Garamond. They are set in an 11pt face with 16pt leading.

Printed in the United States of America
by Bookmasters, Inc., Ashland, OH
first printing, April 2012

Publisher's Cataloging-in-Publication Data

Park, Sarah Dunning.
    What it is is beautiful : honest poems for
    mothers of small children / Sarah Dunning Park.
    p. cm.
    ISBN 978-1-933339-59-7

    1. Motherhood --Poetry.
    2. Mother and child --Poetry.
    3. Mothers --Poetry.
    4. American poetry --21st century.
    5. Women --Poetry.
    I. Title.

    PR9199.3.P337 W48 2012
    811/.54 – dc23   2012937149

Peace Hill Press • 18021 The Glebe Lane • Charles City, VA 23030
peacehillpress.com

CONTENTS

INTRODUCTION

I don't know about you, but I had no idea that becoming a parent would affect my brain as much as it did. We had three babies in three years, and suddenly my life boiled down to pure survival.

I've often told myself to just slog through these days—washing faces, reading stories, saying bedtime prayers. There is a sweetness to it all, which I can usually remember, once everyone's asleep and the house is finally still.

I began writing these poems two years ago, when our twins were three years old and our firstborn was six. I longed to re-engage my brain and my heart with the work of mothering. I needed to discover what was poetic about this overwhelmingly repetitive life.

This book is the beginning of that journey. I'd be honored if you joined me.

– Sarah
April 2012

WELCOME TO FACEBOOK

She wrote on my wall:
i luv mama
(which melted my heart)
but it took forty minutes
of sustained elbow grease
to coax the crayon off.

She poked me
over and over
after crawling into bed
with cold feet
and a sagging diaper
(at six in the morning).

"I'm not your friend anymore!"
she shrieked savagely
after I put her in time-out
for the third time—
I'm thinking, maybe I should join
the real thing?

OBSTACLE COURSE

Last night when I lay
sleepless, thinking,
I turned my problems
from back to front,
then front to back,
trying through worry
to wear them down
to nothing.

If anything,
I only made them
loom larger, by slipping
one next to another,
matching craggy edges
until I had fashioned
an insurmountable
wall.

Today I find
they are neither
worn to dust nor
mortared together;
one by one, they crop out
through the morning.
And as I meet them,
I huff and sigh and whine.

Yet I recall the first
evening of summer camp
when I was fourteen—
we leapt over fallen trees,
grabbed for rough rope ladders,
splashed through mud pits
in the dark.

We laughed raucously
in the face of each hurdle,
and we emerged
from our challenge
soaked but exhilarated,
with skinned knees
and new best friends.

So tomorrow I vow
to try this: the child who
shakes me awake
is the day's starting
pistol, and I will leap up
with vigor, unfazed
by my handicap
of inadequate sleep.

Later I will brave
the oven of our minivan
to maneuver squirming children
into buckles and boosters—
without once losing my cool.

And that evening I will dance
around mounds of laundry,
as I head to my desk
to confront with boldness
the dark recesses
of our perpetually
unbalanced
checkbook.

LOOKING FORWARD
TO A LANYARD

"She gave me life and milk from her breasts,
and I gave her a lanyard."
— Billy Collins, "The Lanyard"

The other day I was reading aloud a story
on the sofa, one warm body on my lap
and another leaning into the curve of my arm,
each of us lost in the satisfying sway of the rhyme,
when one of them suddenly turned to me
and held out her hand—at first, appearing empty
but on closer inspection revealing
a hard-won smear of mucus.

Here, Mom, she said, in full trust
that I would eagerly receive her love offering,
just as I do when one of them says, *Can you take this?*
and presents, like a perfect crescent moon,
a sliver of fingernail for my keeping.
Or, *This is for you!*—handing me
a band-aid that has long since
served its purpose.

These days, I wonder about my own purpose
while keeping tissues handy at all times

and letting my purse bulge with earnest gifts
like rocks and folded scraps of paper.
And in my idle moments I try out thoughts
of a future life, when the children will know
a glorious level of independence,
allowing them to braid long thin plastic strips
at summer camp, without me.

FOUR-YEAR-OLD NINJA

You hop from black square to black square,
focus fixed on missing the quicksand river
of matte beige floor tile.

The bit by the door is always dicey—
you skitter along the dark border,
leap over the perilous metal grate,

grunt with effort and approval
to meet unbroken pavement
and solid stone—

but ahead is a troubling crack;
it cuts across the path,
rearing a concrete tsunami of sure ruin,

yet you skim over it,
touch down miraculously on the next slab,
then bound over each parallel break,
evenly spaced as if made for your stride,

letting you go, no holds barred,
to run for the cool safety
of the grassy sea.

ODE TO OUR MINIVAN

We are driving you
into the ground,
and you keep taking it,
or us, really, along with our
travel mugs, orphaned socks
and cracker crumbs.

Behind your back, I admit,
we dream of our next vehicle:
privacy glass, better gas mileage,
maybe even a sunroof—
but what I wouldn't give
just for power windows!

Your decline is clearest
when I ease you out of
snug parking spaces
or struggle to merge with cars
flying by on the
highway;

tight turns reduce you
to confused stuttering,
while a trip on the Interstate
makes you cough and lurch,
eager to please
but slow to accelerate.

You are not without your
subtle forms of protest:
one day, you up and decided
not to make cold air, except
on HIGH (and if the stars
are aligned).

So now we drive with the windows
down, the humid air in our ears,
and above us your waving flag
of loose ceiling fabric,
faithfully billowing
and flapping.

THE TROUBLE WITH GRASS

The grass is always greener
in those unknown lawns,
where children with
perpetually brushed hair
tussle good-naturedly,
their mother watching
with pride and delight
from a kitchen window,
the evening's hearty stew
simmering on a
gleaming stove.

But the stove I know
wears a greasy patina
encrusted with old spills,
and I stand beside it, stirring,
as if my post there
will protect me from being
required to mediate
the fight erupting outside
between crabby kids
on the weed-ridden grass—
which already needs
mowing again.

IRL

On days when the kids are bored,
they drag themselves to me
on feeble legs, staggering
under the load of their need
for something to make them
feel alive.

So I kick them outside—
not for the exhilarating effect of nature
(though there is that), but because
the effect of being followed
by a small, whining person
is enough to unhinge
my tired mind.

I close the door with relief
as they run off to the sunlit grass,
and then I take my mind by the hand,
and limp with it to the nearest
screen.

I, too, am starving to feel alive,
and so to take the edge off this hunger
I guzzle a stream of 140-character
blips and blurbs, and then move on

to the meat of e-mail
and blog posts.

Afterward, though,
part of me is still not satisfied,
so I try to re-enter real life
by tidying up the house,
my eyes scanning the pieces of my world
to find what is lovely and worthy
of gratitude.

Sure enough—
late afternoon sun is filling
the window over the kitchen sink
with a golden warmth that hallows
those dry garlic bulbs sending out
withered sprouts on the sill.

My first impulse
is to post a picture
of this redemptive beauty,
for all the world to behold and enjoy—

but I'm rescued
by the racket of the kids
bursting in the door

to announce the unexpected arrival
of our neighbor and her daughter,
who have walked over—
on their feet—
to spend time with us
this sunny day.

KEEPING THE PEACE

I saw it out of the corner of my eye,
noticed its tall, silver form
long before naming it in my mind:
heron. It perched, utterly graceful and
still, on a fallen trunk that sloped down
into the creek we cross over every day.
Fog was rising from the water,
and I wished I could stop the car,
approach quietly with camera in hand,
and somehow arrest the moment—
then lift it, intact, to take with me
as an emblem for the day.

Instead I turned away
to face the road again,
letting the moment flick past
like the flipping of channels,
and swallowing my awareness
that we live in a world with—herons.
The children were slumped behind me,
only just lulled into a dubious harmony
that would no doubt be shattered
if we stopped, or if I called out
for them to notice this marvel,
already now behind us.

I envisioned
three heads swiveling,
eager to broaden their horizons
with the wonders of the natural world.
Then I pictured a careless elbow
clipping a seatmate on the chin,
and two sets of hands clawing
at the sibling with the prime view—
of this *animal*
who has had the good sense to freeze
as we go barreling past.

No, I decided
(and it felt ungenerous):
today I would choose to keep
this emblem of peace to myself,
not sharing it with them directly,
but thereby preserving
the absence of conflict in the backseat,
and the heron's solitary breakfast,
and perhaps most important,
that rare jewel—peace of mind—
for me.

BOOK LEARNING

It unfolded so fast
past the hour of the nap
they never take:
one kid goaded the other,
who naturally sank her teeth
in the arm of her foe.

All I could think
was that justice
must be meted out,
and I'm supposed to do it.
But I stood still,
paralyzed—

not by the shrill howl
or the shaky hiccups,
but by the conflicting
voices of well-intentioned
parenting books

(with their absolute
confidence, catchy titles,
and celebrity review blurbs),

each forbidding
a different course
of action:

Don't let it slide;
she'll become
a holy terror!
Don't spank her;
she'll choose violence
to solve her troubles!
Don't pay her extra attention;
she'll learn to act out
to get more!
Don't banish her to her room;
she'll multiply her feelings
of isolation!

So to quiet all the voices,
I yelled at my holy terror,
then wrapped my arms
around her, and
together
we bawled.

ALREADY BUT NOT YET

I have already
run the dishwasher,
put away every
squeaky-clean plate
and sparkling glass;

but I have not yet
tackled the leaning tower
of soggy cereal bowls,
or that pan,
thick with bacon fat.

I have already
pulled warm, snapping towels
out of the dryer and into
my arms, folded them
in neat stacks;

but I have not yet
sorted the piles of soiled
clothes, or washed them
of their stains and
ripe smells.

I have already
drawn my children near,
tucked hair behind their ears,
told them how much
I love them;

but I have not yet
made it through a day
loving perfectly,
free of discontent, guilt,
or fear.

DINNER AT HOME

The work of the day
is over—
but there is still
the matter of
dinner.

Sometimes,
we succumb
to the drive-thru—
scarfing burgers
in the car,
grease dripping down
the backs of our hands.
Throwing french fries
to appease the backseat.
My stomach tenses up
from suspense, bracing
for the next bite, gulp,
or pothole in the road.

Rare are the nights
we eat out, without kids.
I wait for it all day, letting
my thirst for red wine
and hunger for red meat
grow without apology.

I savor the ordering
of food prepared
by other hands;
you feast on the distance
from our sink of dishes.

But most evenings
find us at home,
pulling together a meal
out of something old
and something new.
Papers must be pushed aside,
projects relocated.
I call up the stairs to
come eat, right this minute!

From the hungry sprinters
to the stragglers
reluctantly parting
with toys, books
or screens,
we find our seats
at the table,
bow our heads.
We take,
and we eat.

NIGHT RUMMAGING

"It is the nightly custom of every good mother after her children are asleep to rummage in their minds and put things straight for the next morning, repacking into their proper places the many articles that have wandered during the day."

— J.M. Barrie, *Peter Pan*

I crack the door
to noisy mouth breathing
and see her head thrown back,
face slack-jawed,
cheeks baby-full.

Her limbs are improbably
arranged, an elbow up there,
legs curving behind and back,
as if in mid-spring
to the moon.

Today she stared me down
when I issued a command
and then crumpled
when I finally
lost it.

Now her floor is littered
with wadded socks,
the day's smeary shirt,
a pair of pants pulled clear through
to inside out.

I leave them there;
this moment must not be
for my straightening hands.
I merely breathe in
the uncanny peace,

wordlessly asking
for such peace to dwell
in every drawer
of her mind

and exhaling my gratitude
for making it to this point,
when I get to right
the ransacked corners
of mine.

THEIR EYES ALL AGLOW

What, I wonder,
will they remember
from their childhoods?
If everything experienced
is somehow stored—
stitched into the brain's cortical folds
like a heap of colorful rags
carefully braided and coiled
to make the rug underfoot—
which bits and pieces of memory
will present face-up,
to be felt and seen
and trod upon daily?

I would happily tinker with their minds—
to gently tuck out of reach the memories
of times I snapped at them in anger,
or to bring forward and shore up
their recollection of the days
when all was peaceful,
and love imbued every word.

But I can't control their minds
—nor mine, tonight,
as I snuff out a stub of candle
on our table, and its smoking wick
and heady scent bring on a wave
of remembering I didn't expect:
the feel of a Christmas Eve
when it's late and I am little,
full to bursting with rich food
and my wild impatience
for the morning.

RX

It hit me,
helping my listless kid into the backseat
and then reaching, tissue in hand,
to swipe at her sister's runny nose:
It's impossible to stop.

Her incessant stuffiness, yes,
and that junky cough that won't quit—
but even more, it's impossible to stop
this cycle of constant motion.

I thought all this
while shifting into reverse
and tapping at the map on my phone
and passing a sippy cup to the back
and unwrapping a piece of red candy
masquerading as medicinal balm
for my sore throat.

The sloughed-off wrapper landed softly
among the library books beside me,
but the lozenge's marketing slogan
kept looping through my head:

The show must go on,
it urged, or perhaps warned,
since I felt a sense of deep foreboding
that our show was teetering
on the brink of collapse.

Still, the car raced forward
toward the bland medical office building
where we would join the universal
meet and greet for our germs
and theirs—

to connect briefly
with the kind doctor
who, in a different era,
would have entered into
the intimate domain of our home
to take it all in,
and then thoughtfully scrawl
our needed prescription:
Slow down.

LET THERE BE YES

I say *no* to them all the time:
No, you may not eat candy bars for breakfast,
color pictures on the carpet,
wear your tutu to the store again.
And stop blowing bubbles in your milk,
or abandoning your warm bed
after I've tucked you in.

Perhaps it's the wisdom of age,
or that this is not their full-time gig,
but their grandmothers have another way:
Yes, let's make projects with plenty of glitter and paint,
matching costumes for you and your bear,
hot chocolate for watching movies
on a Saturday morning in June.

I decide to try it myself,
tentatively—*Sure*, I suppose
we can bring out the modeling clay today.
So we spread an old vinyl cloth on the table,
and dump the box that holds baggies of red and black,
blue, green, and yellow. From my post in the kitchen,
I watch them settle in to their work.

It's quiet; no one complains
of boredom or hunger
or cunningly-orchestrated breaches of room security
carried out by little sisters. The only requests
are for assistance rolling up an errant sleeve
or for a toothpick to carve out fine details
and at last, the artist's signature.

As she bends over her masterpiece
to scratch the letters of her name,
I understand what it is my mother must know
when she says *yes* to these young creators:
we are wired to make, and we can make
trouble, or we can make goodness and art
and meaning and sustenance and play.

Many thanks to Grandma Roxy, Mimi,
and Aunt Evie, for saying 'yes' to our kids.

TRIO

(pianissimo) Mama,
pretend I'm a butterfly
named Lyla, a little
purple butterfly who
lives among the
(mezzo-forte) *Mommy,*
I learned the coolest
thing! We made it in
school today and you
need to come see how
(fortissimo) MAMA!
I NEED YOU NOW,
RIGHT HERE AT THE
POTTY! (continuing
in counterpoint)
Mom Mom Mom,

come see, I'm gonna try
MAMA! I NEED TO BE
then get pollen, Mama, and fly
WIPED NOW! *Mom,*
I folded on these lines
WIPE ME, MOMMY!
to my nest up high,
actually now I'm a bird
named Ly—(crescendo)
MAMA! I. AM. POOPY!
—la; chicka-dee-dee
-DEE *Watch out, Mommy,*
watch out, here comes my airp—
POOPY! PLEASE WIPE ME!
Mama—MAMA—
MOMMY!

MOM JEANS

They almost made me gag
as a teen, their pleated
poufs in the front,
ample haunch-girding
acreage in the back,
all in just the wrong
shade of blue.

I dismissed them outright
as pegging the woman
contained within
as a forty-something mother
who'd given up on life,
namely, fashion
(and then I carefully
pegged my own pair
at the ankle).

Now I am a mom
who wears jeans
(the same pair every day),
chosen for comfort
and their gracious overlooking
of the lapse I like to attribute
to a physician-ordered
caesarean.

And I don't peg
pants anymore—
I stagger through life,
reeling from the weight of being
responsible for other people,
and the bewildering
burden of choosing
between a bootcut
and a straight leg.

A SPRING ISSUE

Standing in line
at the grocery checkout,
my eye slides over your glossy cover

and I imagine kicking back
in a quiet room at home,
sunlit air from the window
fluttering your bright pages.

I would quietly feed on
your inspiring concepts
for dining al fresco, plus
one hundred great ways
to bring back the romance
(and still get dinner on the table).

Actually dinner
is burning in the oven
while I fitfully pore over
page after page
of simulated perfection,
my brain racked by the effort
of mentally tallying these things
I surely need:

a battery of skin-care
potions to charm my face
into a pristine, even poreless
surface and a new wardrobe
that flatters my assets
while suiting my age
(as well as resisting stains)
and that Viking range
with granite countertops
where I'll roast local lamb
or raptly dice Vidalias
and the end of each day
dedicated to meditative yoga,
to targeting and toning and
releasing stress and toxins—

not to mention toxic emotions,
risen to a high boil
within my ravenous heart,
now bleating for a taste of the flawless
(which I think I've just beheld
here in your artful pages).

Little can I do
but dish up our lenten meal
(peas and potatoes)

and then I will sacrifice you,
sham of the perfect,
to the trash, sprinkling you
with the crumbs of tonight's
charred fish sticks.

WHAT IT IS IS BEAUTIFUL

I'd really had it with the mess,
the way there wasn't a single clear surface
to deflect the meager winter light,
but only piles of haphazard papers
made up of macaroni crafts
purporting to be flat.

Clothing was flung on the floor,
from jackets in the front hall
to a trail of socks and sweaters
as the kids molted
on their way to the kitchen.

I stalked through it,
seething over the futility of a to-do list
featuring anything other than
Pick up after people
—when the corner of a toy
dug into my foot.

I staggered, and blinked,
and then it was in my hand,
my arm wound back,
ready to hurl the offending plastic
straight into the trash—

but something stopped me.
Maybe it was the thought of my child
careening through the house,
wearing a million-dollar smile
and this lego creation on her head,

or maybe it was just my usual exhaustion.
I flopped down on the sofa,
raised the toy to my face,
and peered through.

The makeshift lenses
were sticky and clouded
and smelled suspiciously of banana.
But a vision of the room entered in with a glow,
and I leaned forward,
incredulous:

A massive bear
stood where our dining table had been,
offering his broad back for our daily rounds
of dinner and homework.

Below him,
the floor was a slick pane of ice
spread out in all directions.

As I watched, one of the kids
came running in from the hall,
then did a swift drop
and slid the length of the room
on her knees.

I laughed and stood up,
set the goggles on a shelf:
dinner wasn't getting made
by this magic, and my ice skater
would soon be clamoring for a meal.

So I picked my way across the cold floor,
kicking lumps of clothing into corners
to clear the rink, and stopping only
to give our messy table
an affectionate pat.

I considered attempting
a knee slide right up to the stove,
but instead drew a long breath
and stepped to my post—
to undertake a task from my list
and forage in a fridge of leftovers
for items I could transform
into a feast.

ABOUT THE AUTHOR

Sarah Dunning Park lives in rural Virginia with her husband, Charlie, their eight-year-old daughter (Lucy), and their five-year-old twin girls (Frances and Kate). She is a freelance illustrator, mapmaker, and poet. She's been writing poems since she was 7.

You can learn more about Sarah, sign up for new poem updates, and find out how to connect with her on Twitter, Facebook, and by e-mail, at sarahdunningpark.com